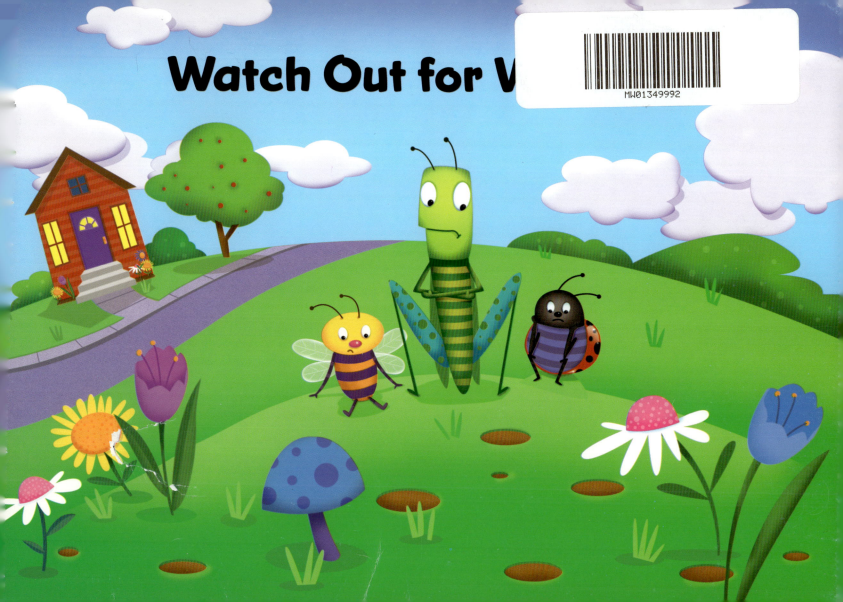

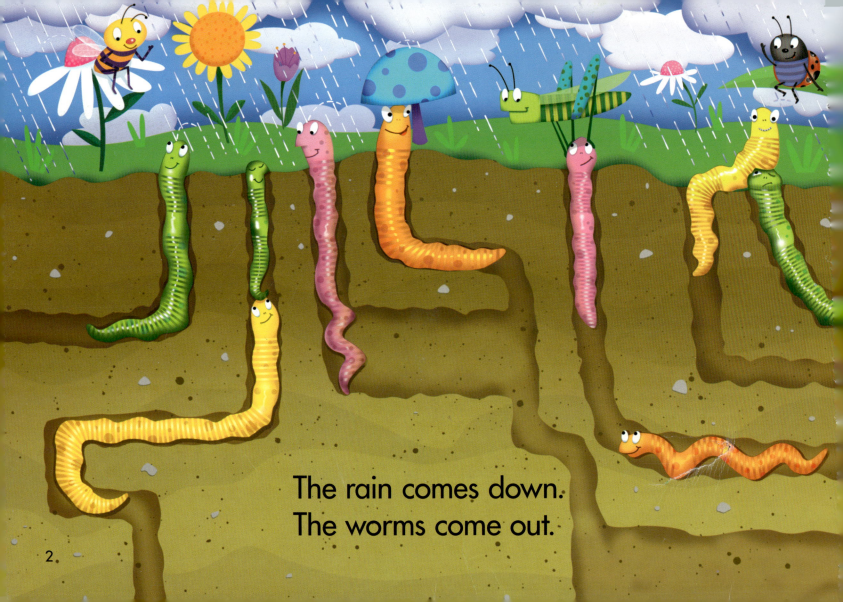

The rain comes down.
The worms come out.

Wiggle, wiggle, wiggle, wiggle.
Worms all about.
*Watch out for worms.
Watch out for worms!*

Worms on the sidewalk.
Worms on the stair.

Wiggle, wiggle, wiggle, wiggle.
Worms everywhere!
Watch out for worms.
Watch out for worms!

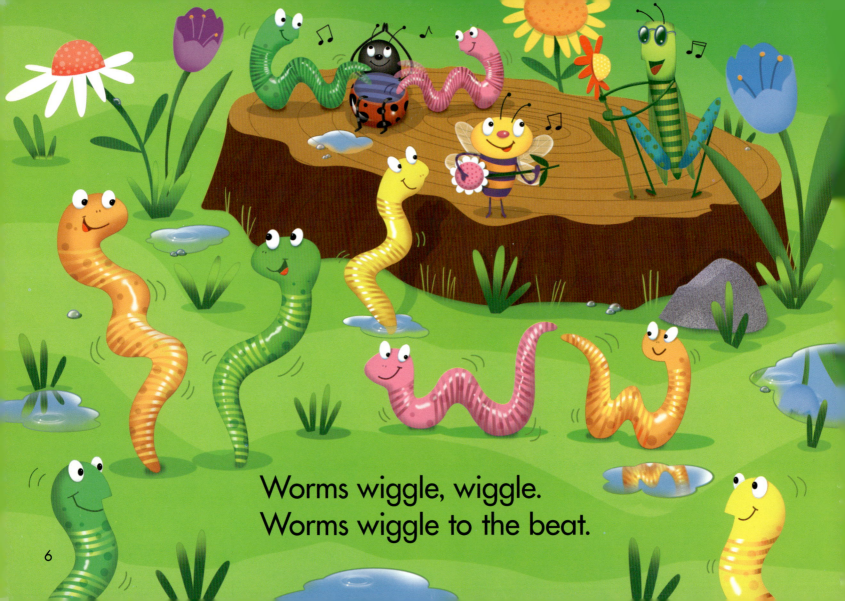

Worms wiggle, wiggle.
Worms wiggle to the beat.

Worms wiggle, wiggle.
They don't have feet.